How to Build a Relationship with the God of Your Understanding

JANE BEACH

How to Build a Relationship with the God of Your Understanding

Part One: Start Where You Are

A Personal Workbook

KENOS PRESS

An Imprint of Six Degrees Publishing Group

KENOS PRESS
an Imprint of Six Degrees Publishing Group
5320 Macadam Avenue, Suite 100
Portland, Oregon 97239

ISBN: 978-0-9856048-9-9

eBook ISBN: 978-1-942497-00-4
US Library of Congress Control Number
2014955745

Front Cover Design: Judy Bullard
Editorial & Design Supervision: Denise C. Williams

Inquiries: Publisher@SixDegreesPublishing.com

KENOS PRESS and its logo are trademarks of Six Degrees Publishing Group

Published in the United States of America

Printed simultaneously in the United States of America,
the United Kingdom and Australia

1 3 5 7 9 10 8 6 4 2

You do not need to know precisely what is happening,
or exactly where it is all going.
What you need is to recognize the possibilities
and challenges offered by the present moment,
and to embrace them with courage, faith and hope.

—THOMAS MERTON

CONTENTS

Introduction   1

How to Use this Personal Workbook   5

ONE: **JANE'S STORY: FROM ATHEIST TO MINISTER**   9

*Whether you believe in the God of your understanding or not,
it believes in you. It is simply waiting for you to notice it.*

    Questions for contemplation / 12
    What My Higher Power Feels Like Today /15

TWO: **RELIGION OR SPIRITUALITY? MAKE A FRESH START**   17

*Despite your childhood conditioning, in this moment you get to
make a choice about what you believe today – a fresh start.*

    Questions for contemplation / 19
    Sensing the Presence / 21

THREE: **WHAT ARE YOU LISTENING TO: EGO OR YOUR INNER WISDOM?**   23

*Are you paying attention to the mind chatter of your ego or the
divine direction of your own inner wisdom?*

    Questions for contemplation / 26
    What ego's fear-based negativity *feels* like. / 28
    What my inner wisdom's faith-based optimism *feels* like. / 29

FOUR: **PRETEND YOUR HIGHER POWER IS REAL**   **31**

*You are a powerful creator! Use your imagination to create
a relationship with a Higher Power that works for you.*

Questions for contemplation /34
10 Attributes that define my Higher Power / 35
How the God of my understanding is
showing up in my life / 37

FIVE: **BECOME WILLING TO TRUST**   **39**

*Become willing to believe that you are divinely loved by a God
who adores you. It's your invitation to trust that life is for you,
simply because you exist.*

Questions for contemplation / 41
My Affirmation / 44

SIX: **UNDERSTANDING SPIRITUAL LAWS**   **47**

*What you believe becomes true for you. Understanding how spiritual
laws work opens up a whole new realm of possibility!*

Questions for contemplation / 50
15 Simple Things / 52
How Self-Care is Affecting My Life / 53

SEVEN: **PEELING THE ONION SOMETIMES MAKES YOU CRY**   **55**

*Peeling away the layers of the onion to discover the beauty of who
you really are brings up negative emotions that are waiting
to be noticed and accepted.*

Questions for contemplation / 58
My Onion / 61

EIGHT: **CHOOSING HAPPINESS**   **63**

*Choosing a life of happiness invites you to see through the eyes
of possibility instead of despair, opting for peace over drama,
releasing negative beliefs.*

Questions for contemplation / 66
I'm Grateful / 68

NINE: **DIVINE DISCONTENT**   71

*Divine discontent surfaces when things that used to bring you
pleasure are no longer satisfying. It's a signal that change
is at hand.*

    Questions for contemplation / 74
    Celebrating Change – One Small Step at a Time / 78

TEN: **GROWING YOUR FAITH**   81

*As your faith grows you'll find a new appreciation for you. You'll
discover that you are worthy of living the life of your dreams!*

    Questions for contemplation / 83
    Today this is ME / 86
    What I Believe Could Be Possible / 88
    Evidence of Change / 91

SHARING WHAT'S BEEN REVEALED TO YOU: 105

Guidelines for group meetings

FACILITATOR GUIDES FOR EACH CHAPTER   109

Step-by-step suggestions for the facilitator
    First Meeting / 109
    One . . . 110
    Two . . . 112
    Three . . . 115
    Four . . . 117
    Five . . . 119
    Six . . . 121
    Seven . . . 123
    Eight . . . 125
    Nine . . . 127
    Ten . . . 129

ABOUT JANE BEACH   133

A Note from Jane Beach

This book is about you!

You read lots about what others think, but when it comes right down to it, all that matters is what you think.

This is your personal workbook with no right or wrong answers, a journal in which to contemplate your thoughts, opinions, questions, revelations, and everything that comes in-between.

∼

INTRODUCTION

The God of your understanding is alive and well in every aspect of your life, just waiting for your attention. It's the sun warming your face, the breeze touching your cheek, and the earth under your feet. It's what grows your fingernails, beats your heart, breathes your every breath and reminds you that it's okay to put yourself first. It knows you intimately and loves you unconditionally, regardless of what your life looks like. No matter what you've ever thought, said, or done, you are the Beloved's cherished one.

This workbook is designed to be a safe haven where you can relax into your personal relationship with a God that's real to *you*, whatever you call Him/Her/It. If at this point in your life, you are seeking a deeper relationship with your Higher Power—even though you're unsure of what that Higher Power *is*—you're in the right place! Here you get to make it up! Because the Divine Presence is pure Love, it wants nothing more than for you to be happy! Because it is everything, it will be to you what you want it to be.

I call the Presence "it" because I know it as energy, an energy of Love that's gentle and comforting, and at the same time, powerful and wise. When I'm afraid, it wraps itself around me almost like a soft cocoon, letting me know that I'm safe, reminding me that I have my own courage within me. When I'm grieving, it folds me in its tender embrace, like a newborn swaddled in the softest blanket. When I'm resentful, angry, or judgmental, it holds me until I'm done feeling my negativity until, once again, I'm so filled with its love that I remember that I too, am love. This same energy is within me as my own inner wisdom . . . my soul . . . my personal cheerleader.

෴ ෴ ෴

There are lots of names for God, and you get to choose which ones work for you. I call it Love, the Beloved, the God that adores me, the greatest Love of all, the One, Creator, Presence and anything else that suits my fancy at the time. Because the Beloved knows me intimately, it already knows what I mean—my names for it are for my own clarity. No matter whether you call it Spirit, Infinite Intelligence, Life, Source, Universe, Higher Power, Harry or Harriet, it's all the same thing—the same love, peace, joy and power that adores you completely and forever, just because you exist. As you get to know it in your own way you will come to know yourself more deeply; you will begin to understand the glory of your worth . . . the beauty of who you truly are.

As you work through this personal workbook you'll discover that as a spiritual being, you are made from the same stuff as your Higher Power—peace, love, wisdom and joy. As a spiritual being having a human experience, your life is filled with messiness—words you wish you could take back after blurting them out in frustration, self-doubt when you know it's time to move forward, memories of victimization born from past experiences, and general feelings of, "I'm not good enough." The purpose of the work you do here is to realize that:

1. Your human thoughts, feelings and experiences are not wrong. You are not bad. They are simply part of your human experience.

2. Underneath all of those human experiences, you are the very breath of the One that created you; you are the perfection of Life itself.

3. The energy of the greatest Love of all is right smack in the middle of your very human experience, accepting you just as you are, guiding you to your highest happiness.

This—your personal workbook—is about better understanding your relationship with your God and with yourself. The time and attention you give to the work you do here will change the way you move through the world because you'll come to know and appreciate *you* in ways you've never considered. Just stay open. Keep showing up.

Know that you are worth every minute you give to this process of self-discovery.

A couple of suggestions

Treat yourself well as you delve into this workbook. You may want to create a sacred space to do this work, perhaps light a candle and play soft, meditative music as you contemplate a question.

Please have crayons, colored pencils, markers or a child's box of watercolors handy. Sometimes drawing is better than words at capturing feelings.

It's my intention to create such a safe atmosphere for you that you can let down old barriers and relax into your personal relationship with whatever Spirit is to you, allowing it to blossom and grow in a way that feels right to *you*.

~ Jane Beach

HOW TO USE
THIS PERSONAL WORKBOOK

Whether embarking on a new journey to building a relationship with the God of your understanding, or seeking to enhance your current relationship with Him/Her/It, there are many creative ways and settings in which you can use this workbook. Here are some suggestions:

Independently

- Move through the work on your own, at your own pace.

- Set aside time to read the chapter and answer the questions. You may choose to answer one question per day, contemplating it before writing down your thoughts.

With a trusted friend

- You and a friend can do the work independently and then call each other to discuss how you're doing.

- Share the changes you see in yourselves and your lives as a result of this work.

In small groups, either online or in person

- This is a great opportunity to meet with friends or others of like mind, either online or in group settings.

- At the end of this workbook you'll find a section called "Sharing What's Been Revealed to You," which provides guidelines for group meetings.

12-step recovery

- A useful tool for sponsors and their sponsees, this workbook provides a powerful journey for anyone in recovery who is searching for a personal relationship with their Higher Power.

- Use for individual or group study in rehab or addiction recovery programs.

Churches and spiritual centers

- This workbook works well as a class textbook. The class facilitator can manage the class discussions using the guidelines in the "Sharing What's Been Revealed to You" and "Facilitator Guides for Each Chapter" sections.

Book study groups

- As a fine addition to your regular book study meeting, this book is sure to spark much conversation. Facilitation is easy with the guidelines in the "Sharing What's Been Revealed to You" section which begins on page 105.

Retreats

- Retreats can be centered on the material in this workbook, as groups of people deepen their relationship with a God that's personal to each. Together the group celebrates the changes within themselves and each other as the result of participating in the retreat.

- The "Facilitator Guides for Each Chapter" included in this book can be used by the retreat facilitator to guide the discussions.

Prayer partners

- Enlisting the support of a prayer partner opens up an avenue to healing as you move through this process of self-discovery.

Make it up!

- Use your imagination and come up with whatever learning experience works best for you!

Your workbook is designed as a journal in which to contemplate *your* thoughts, opinions, questions, and insights. However you choose to use it is perfect!

∼ Notes ∼

ONE

JANE'S STORY:
FROM ATHEIST TO MINISTER

As a lifelong atheist, if anyone would have told me that one day I would become a minister, I would have laughed! For the first fifty years of my life I never talked about God because why talk about something that doesn't exist?

Then something happened. In 1998 my thirty-year marriage was crumbling, and I finally had an incentive to return to Al-Anon (a 12-step program of recovery for families and friends of alcoholics). I had tried Al-Anon twenty-five years earlier, but I couldn't find a meeting that wasn't centered on the concept of a Higher Power, so I quit. Now at this low point, I took a good look at my life and asked, "Is this it? Is this *all* my life is about?" For the first time in years I considered *myself*, which was very different than my usual 'take care of everyone else' mentality. At that moment, a tiny crack in my defiant, defensive armor appeared, a window of opportunity for the God of my understanding to make itself known in a way that I would notice. After asking the question, "Is this *all* my life is about?" the very next thought that came up was, "It's time to return to Al-Anon." It surprised me, but it also somehow made sense; I knew I needed to do it. Today I've learned that God-messages are often a brand new thought that comes from somewhere deep within me, which is exactly what happened in this instance. At the time all I knew was that if I wanted to fix *me*, I needed to show up in the rooms of recovery.

I dove right in, telling my new 12-step friends, "I can make the coffee, put out the literature, and clean up; I just can't do that God-thing." They grinned and said, "Keep coming back!" Somehow I knew to follow their advice—to show up, stay open, listen and learn, so that's what I did.

My sponsor taught me about using a God Box, which is a sacred container designed to give your worries to your Higher Power. You write down your needs and then place the note into the box. By giving it over to God you're supposed to be done worrying: "Let Go and Let God." Most people seal their box closed so they won't be tempted to open it up to look at their problems again, thereby 'taking them back.' God Boxes are generally decorated with pictures, symbols and words of personal significance and then put in a special place. I was really struggling with the whole Higher Power concept—my snippy atheist brain in full rebellion. While I agreed to make a God Box, it was beyond my capabilities to make it 'sacred'—heck, I didn't even use words like 'sacred!' I made mine out of a shoebox, taped it closed with duct tape, cut a slit in the top and threw it on the closet shelf. There it sat for months, unused.

On July 4, 1998, I awakened with a feeling of agitation that I couldn't shake. What was up? Usually I was pretty even tempered, but on this day I felt really irritated for no particular reason, and I wanted the feeling to go away. For the first time I used my God Box—what was there to lose? I didn't begin the note with "Dear God" because I didn't believe in God; instead I wrote "I need tolerance." With an almost defiant *Whatcha gonna to do about this?* I stuck the note in the God Box, threw it back up on the closet shelf and got on with my day. Instead of getting better, my day got worse! I couldn't make that annoyed, agitated feeling go away. I felt completely out of control. So much for trusting God!

It turned out that the whole thing was a big God-setup, because that evening I had my first conscious awareness of the God of my understanding. I used sleep as an escape in those days, and finally I decided to watch a bit of TV before escaping to bed, to sleep, and maybe things would be better in the morning. The moment I sat down to watch TV, a feeling of peace like I had never known before enveloped me. It was incredible! I knew what it felt like to be peaceful, but this was much more than that. Gentle, loving energy filled me and also wrapped itself around me, like that soft cocoon I mentioned earlier. It moved very slowly, just enough so that I was aware of its presence. I silently asked, *What is this?* barely breathing for fear it would go away. I didn't understand it, but I wanted it. I focused on it, leaning into it, breathing it in. In the fullness of this inexplicable great peace, I could feel a shift; something within me was relaxing, changing, awakening.

I went to bed, slept amazingly well, and in the morning that same unbelievable peace was still there. And there was more—now there was also an incredible feeling of profound love. It was everywhere, in my heart and behind my eyes, so that everywhere I looked, I saw through the eyes of love! Then I got it! I finally understood that what I was feeling was what people call God. Softly, gently and with great purpose, the greatest Love of all had entered my life in a way that I could recognize. In an instant I knew that I was profoundly loved and always had been, no matter what I had ever said or done. I also knew that all this time this great Love had been patiently waiting for me to notice it.

I sobbed with the enormity of this simple and yet powerful revelation, drenching my pillow with tears that washed away years of disbelief. In the process I was held by the one I now call the Beloved. I could actually feel Love's presence on my skin, in my hair, and even in the covers—it *was* the covers! I knew it had always been with me and that I was cherished just because I exist. I was cradled in its love as if I were the most precious infant. It wasn't until later in the day that I remembered the God Box, my reluctant first step toward the shift in consciousness that allowed my Higher Power in.

❧ ❧ ❧

From that point forward my life was forever changed. Without any intellectual understanding of God, my walk with the Beloved has been purely experiential. Beginning with that first experience, my relationship with a presence I knew as pure Love became the most important part of my life.

When I didn't know what to do, I learned that there was a part of me that did know. It was as if the Beloved had given me the opportunity to know myself.

"My treasured one,
    I give you the gift of recognizing your own beauty
        . . . your own perfection.
    It is the part of you that is of me.
    You are me and I am you."

This journal is about getting to know *you* in a new way. It's about discovering and fostering a relationship with the God of *your* understanding—that great Love which is forever courting you. Experiencing the God of your understanding may be closer than you think. It's where you are this very minute, looking for a way to catch your attention. As your eyes dance over these words and your heart stirs with possibility, it loves you beyond measure. As you build a personal relationship with it in a way that's real for you, your life will change. Let's begin!

~

Take some quiet time to contemplate the following questions, answering them with what's true for you today. Your answers may change tomorrow, and again the day after that. The process of self-discovery often comes with little bits of awareness. If you don't have this workbook with you when you have a new realization, keep a small notebook handy to jot it down. Everything counts!

At this point in my life, what is my relationship with the God of my understanding?

_____

_____

What does it feel like? Is it love, peace, strength, wisdom, fun?

_____

_____

How do I sense its presence—in music, nature, my pet, a friend's smile?

_____

_____

What do I believe is true about God/Life? If struggle with this question I can ask: What do I _want_ to believe is true about God/Life?

_____

_____

What are my spiritual needs? Do I need something that I can count on in difficult situations? Do I need to know that I matter in the world? Do I need to learn to love and appreciate myself? Do I need to know that my Higher Power is real?

_____

_____

What questions do I have?

_____

_____

Try this: Imagine what it feels like to be in the presence of someone who cherishes you. Their face lights up at the sight of you! It doesn't matter whether you cry or make messes; they love you just as you are. Now magnify this feeling a million percent and you'll get a sense of the magnitude of the Beloved's love for you.

Either draw or find illustrations that are symbolic of what your Higher Power *feels* like today, or what you *want* your Higher Power to feel like in your life—walking on the beach, your pet's fur, waking up after a good night's sleep, holding hands with someone who cares about you.

∼ What My Higher Power Feels Like Today ∼

TWO

RELIGION OR SPIRITUALITY?
MAKE A FRESH START

The power and presence of Love is where you are this moment. It knows who you are, and it consistently seeks your attention in the smallest of ways: turning your face to the sun just to feel its warmth, enjoying the first bite of your favorite food, the song on the radio that makes you want to sing out loud, a feeling of peace amidst chaos, or your gratitude for a good night's sleep. In endless ways it whispers to you, "I'm here, and I adore you. I want you to be happy. I'm at the core of your desire to laugh out loud, notice something beautiful, or give yourself credit for a job well done. I'm the relief when you finally release your tears, tell the truth, or let go of trying to control a situation that doesn't belong to you. I am here, and I love you."

Wherever you are, at all times, the God of your understanding is right there, so why does it seem so elusive? Why doesn't everyone notice it? I have a hunch that for many, the answer lies in their childhood conditioning—what they were taught about God. Think back to when you were a child; were you raised in a particular religion or religious philosophy? Did it make sense to you? Did it bring you peace? Did it bring peace to the adults around you? Often adults are taught *about* God but struggle with *knowing* God. It can be very confusing to a little kid!

There are subtle differences between religion and spirituality. The world is filled with many diverse religions and faith traditions, each with its own ideas about God/

Deity and corresponding rules for moral behavior. Religions have specific beliefs that tend to be exclusive to that group. Their defined approaches to life are outlined, which helps their followers align their own ethical behavior with the expectations of the group. As the group follows the outlined doctrines, one person's answered prayer uplifts others and strengthens the beliefs of the whole. Together, their faith grows.

Spirituality is more of a personal thing; it's about belonging to *you* and to the whole of life. It's inclusive of all religions, as well as those who are agnostic or atheist. Spirituality is about personal transformation, opening up to the idea that the glory of God is within you . . . your own spiritual essence. Your beliefs are evidenced in the way you live your life, rather than what you are taught. On a spiritual path you tend to learn *how* to think, not *what* to think. The awakening to your spiritual nature may take place in a moment of inspiration while gazing at a magnificent sunset, while listening to music, reading encouraging words, hearing a message you know is meant just for you, or a synchronistic Aha! moment that reminds you that life is a mystery. For some, like me, the awakening comes in the form of a single awakening experience.

Many people who were raised in a particular religion find comfort and fulfillment within the beliefs of that religion, which is great! Sometimes that isn't the case and the person is left with many questions. They may eventually set out to find *something* that they can believe in. Therein lay the shift from religion to spirituality, as they seek a deeper personal relationship with life and with themselves. If you were raised with religious teachings, did those teachings parallel the longings of your own heart? Because we are all beautifully unique, what you heard as a child may or may not have resonated with what you intuitively knew to be true. It's possible that even if your religion currently works well in your life, today you may be looking for a deeper understanding. You're likely doing the work in this workbook because as a spiritual seeker, you're looking for something more.

∾

What was my religion of origin, if any?

_____

_____

Did it work for me? If so, how was it helpful? If not, why not?

_____

_____

What impact does my childhood religious upbringing have on my thoughts about life today?

_____

_____

What other religions, philosophies or teachings have influenced me?

_____

_____

As a child, what name did I call God, if any?

_____

_____

What do I call the God of my understanding today? Do I refer to it as Him, Her or It? (If you're still trying to figure it out, be gentle with yourself—it's all okay!)

_____

_____

Try this: Draw or make a collage of things and situations that help you sense the presence of a Higher Power (perhaps being in nature, the company of friends or those who inspire you, reading spiritual material, feeling grateful, enjoying your favorite activities or hobbies).

∾ Sensing the Presence ∾

THREE

What Are You Listening To: Ego or Your Inner Wisdom?

If you're like me, your mind can get very busy, chattering away about everything! It's like turning the TV to your own personal news channel, one that provides continuous feedback. Your personal commentator gives you input about what you're seeing, who you're with, what happened yesterday, interspersed with commercials to remind you that you're hungry or need to stop for gas. The question becomes, what channel are you tuning in to? Is the newsfeed positive or negative, helpful or harmful? Once you become aware of the difference between the messages of your ego and those of your inner wisdom, your choice of channels will become much clearer!

The ego is an archaic part of the human mind, leftover from the cave man days when fight or flight occurrences were very real, and fear often kept us safe. Today our ego remains fear-driven; it's still trying to keep us safe. The problem is that within the ego's safety zone—our comfort zone—we're stifled, kind of like stashing a toddler in a playpen all day. The minute you even think about setting off on a new adventure your ego yells, *Be careful! There could be danger! You could get hurt! You might not succeed! Don't even try!* Fear sets in and you begin to doubt that you have what it takes to even begin, let alone follow the dream that keeps tugging at your heart.

As a way to protect you, your ego has a 'me against them' mentality that tries to keep you separate from others, since they might disappoint you, decide not to be your friend, or otherwise hurt you with their words or actions. Ego has a critical eye and something to say about everyone and every situation! If you're in a long line at the store and find yourself entertaining complaining thoughts—the cashier is too slow; the store should have more help; you shouldn't need to waste your time like this—you've tuned into your ego channel. If you catch yourself complaining about the tedious preflight process at the airport or the bad drivers on the freeway, you're once again focused on the ego channel—complaining is its specialty!

Your ego's formidable insistence on being right leads you to believe that life is full of obstacles; it's hard and you need to be alert to what could go wrong. Your relationship with yourself is often your biggest hurdle. You hang onto regrets or anger from situations that happened years ago and then beat yourself up because you can't let them go. That self-blame seems to sabotage the very happiness you seek, becoming a vicious cycle. You ask, "What's wrong with me that I can't leave this alone? Why do I keep bringing it up?" as you feel your self-worth take another step backward.

Let's put ego into perspective. In reality it's just a part of your mind that plays the same old negative reruns over and over. The situations may be new, but your response to them doesn't change much. Paying attention to ego's ramblings has become a habit. The good news is that you don't have to listen! Habits are meant to be broken, and you can change the channel! Once you discover the uplifting, empowering messages of your soul—your inner wisdom—you'll begin to tune into a new perspective, one with a positive newsfeed of optimism, gratitude, forgiveness and respect.

ℰꝰ ℰꝰ ℰꝰ

Your soul is the part of you that is of God—it's your divine spark . . . your spiritual essence . . . your inner wisdom . . . your personal cheerleader . . . the one that lights the way when you have no idea what to do next. Because it's made of the same stuff as the Creator, it is love, peace, wisdom, joy, balance, clarity, and all manner of endless possibilities. It's you! It's who you are as a spiritual being. The face you see in the mirror is the spiritual being having a human experience.

Long before I knew God was real my soul was guiding me; I just didn't know it. It's what kept me safe when I put myself in unsafe conditions as a teen. It's what guided me when my kids were struggling, when money was tight, when I tried to find the right words to comfort a friend who was hurting. It's been there all along for you, too. In challenging times, it's what has given you the strength to stay the course, or the wisdom to change directions, or the courage to go after something new.

How do you tell the difference between your soul's message and the mind chatter of your ego? For me the difference is in how it makes me feel. My ego reminds me of past failures and all the reasons I can't do the thing I want to do. Fear sets in, I feel less-than, my stomach knots up and I'm irritable. It pits me against the world because the world is isn't a safe place.

My soul makes me feel worthy and capable—it's my personal cheerleader! Its gentle and encouraging, "You can do it!" shines the light of possibility on each new adventure that nudges me out of my comfort zone. It reminds me that every time I listen to my own best intentions, I proclaim my worth. I may not feel very worthy because of those nagging doubts about failing, but underneath the fear is a vast reservoir of joyous God-Love that absolutely believes in me. I've learned to trust it, even when my ego tells me to run and hide. The world becomes a safe place because I believe that I will know what to do with whatever situation comes my way. My inner wisdom reminds me that my presence on this planet matters and that I'm meant to live a life that's happy, fulfilling and free.

How do you change the channel from ego to your soul's message? It's a process, one that takes time and practice, with lots of room for mistakes, self-care and self-compassion. When you catch yourself complaining, give yourself credit for noticing and then make a conscious decision to think of something positive, perhaps something you're grateful for. It's one small step at a time.

Your spiritual journey invites you to embrace true happiness, which is an inside job. By letting down your human defenses and surrendering into the goodness life has to offer, the naturally harmonious, abundant and loving flow of the universe is set into motion on your behalf. Part of the journey is embracing the invisible. You finally remember that you were born of the greatest Love of all, and that peace is your nature. Instead of trying to change the world around you, you let it be, accepting the call to change yourself. You relax into life instead of fighting it. You gain clarity with every decision you make, creating new avenues to physical and emotional health, and the self-love that opens your eyes to see your connection with the world around you. You attain universal compassion through the experience of accepting one person at a time, beginning with yourself. Instead of seeking happiness, you become the happiness you seek. Your personal walk with your Higher Power creates newfound courage and self-worth, "I can do it. I'm safe. I will know the way." Even when you're afraid, you take the next step and move forward because you've discovered that your soul—your inner wisdom—is the voice you can trust. Welcome to your wisdom channel!

ᥱ

Here I will name five ways that tuning into my ego channel has interfered with my happiness (for example: gossip, complaining, comparing myself to others, playing small, judging myself or another, not trying). What were the circumstances and how did it make me feel?

1. _____

2. _____

3. _____

4. _____

5. _____

Here I will name five ways that the messages I hear on my soul's wisdom channel have championed me (followed my intuition, found my courage, let go of a situation that wasn't good for me, nudged me forward when I thought I couldn't do it, let myself off the hook when I made a mistake). What were the circumstances and how did it feel?

1. _____

2. _____

3. _____

4. _____

5. _____

Am I willing to do my best to stop paying attention to the ego channel, releasing the old patterns of complaining, victimization, and every other negativity that keeps me from living the amazing life I was meant to live?

_____

Am I willing to do my best to tune into the wisdom of my own soul, replacing negativity with my growing optimism?

_____

Try this: Find pictures or draw what fear-based ego-negativity *feels* like. Now find pictures or draw what faith-based optimism *feels* like. Ask yourself, "Which one do I want more of in my life? What do I intend to do about it?

> ∾ What Ego's Fear-Based Negativity *Feels* Like ∾

∾ What My Inner Wisdom's Faith-Based Optimism *Feels* Like ∾

Which one do I want more of in my life—fear or faith? What do I intend to do about it?

FOUR

Pretend Your Higher Power is Real

I t's time to come to the conclusion that you are worthy of all the happiness life has to offer—happiness beyond your wildest expectations! Once you realize you really are cherished by the greatest Love of all that feeling of worthiness will start to kick in. Easier said than done, you might say! There are a couple of ongoing gifts you can give yourself in order to move forward, out of your old thinking and into the new.

Your first gift comes with the acceptance of the idea that your Higher Power is real . . . alive and awake, fully present in every aspect of your life. It's who you are, expressing as you. Your personal relationship with the God of your understanding fosters the beauty of who you are, and who you are is a beautiful thing. No matter what you think of yourself or what your life looks like, you have within you a seed of greatness, the promise of potential, a reminder that you bless the world by being alive today, just as you are.

You may think, *That sounds great, but how do I get there?* That's where your glorious creativity comes in! Remember your active imagination as a child? Bring it back, let it surface, and pretend! Pretend that your Higher Power is real. Pretend it's the air you breathe, the leaves on the trees, the rain on your face, the rainbow after a storm, the music you hear, the food you eat. Pretend it's what moves the blood through your body, beats your heart, and tells your fingernails to grow. See and feel it everywhere!

Pretend that it's *for* you and never against you, wanting only your absolute happiness. Pretend that this great power lives *as you*, so that you will always know what to do and how to do it, no matter the situation.

The circumstances of my life were a struggle when I discovered that the Beloved was real. There were times when I was so frightened that I kept a running commentary with the Beloved, just to feel closer to it:

I'm walking out of the house to go to the meeting. I'm getting into the car, buckling my seatbelt. Now I'm backing out of the driveway. I'll get there in plenty of time. I'll know how to act. I won't react to negativity. You will tell me what to say and how to say it.

I was committed to keeping my focus on my Higher Power. My commitment came from my willingness to pretend that it was right there with me, that it heard every word, even when the words were spoken silently in my head. In the process I discovered that I was right—it was with me every step of the way. Beginning this minute, start using your imagination and pretend that you know the God of your understanding is wherever you are, and watch what happens.

The second gift you can give yourself is an understanding of the power of your own creative mind. At one time it was believed that the Earth was flat, surrounded by water. The fear of going beyond physical boundaries kept people in limitation where they felt safe. When astronomers and courageous seafarers challenged that belief, it opened up a whole new world! Slowly, the urge to discover overtook fear, and humanity moved forward. The same is true as the world discovers and tests out the spiritual laws by which Life creates.

Spiritual laws are predictable, just like the physical laws of gravity, buoyancy, and electricity. Physical laws act the same for everyone; the object falls no matter who drops it; the cork floats regardless of who tosses it into the water, and the light goes on for whoever flips the switch. Likewise, spiritual laws are predictable and work the same for everyone. It doesn't matter who you are, what position you hold in life, or how much money you have; the laws work automatically. The power of your thought sets into motion the circumstances of your life—what you think about you create. If your thoughts are mostly negative, you'll draw more negativity to you. If your thoughts are mostly positive, you'll attract more positive situations. Understanding the creative power of your thought is your opportunity to see past old limitations and move in a brand new direction. When you shift your attitude, the universe senses that shift and sets into motion new experiences in your life. Your change in perspective automatically shifts the possibilities of any situation, creating a new gateway to success.

You may have heard the saying, *misery loves company*. It applies here. Misery will find another miserable person or miserable situation because it loves company! Think of your life as a garden. What seeds are you planting? If you're planting seeds of misery, you will automatically grow people and circumstances that bring misery to you. With each new miserable experience, your thoughts of misery are validated, "I knew this would happen! See, I can't win. I am miserable because _____." The blank is generally filled in with the name of someone who has done you wrong or a challenging situation over which you feel you have no control. Your thoughts often accompany an underlying feeling of victimization. It's a cycle that repeats itself over and over; you are co-creating your own miserable reality with the power of your creative thinking.

The good news is that once you plant a new seed, the results will reflect that change. Plant a seed of gratitude and you'll get more to be grateful for. Plant a seed of friendship and you'll find yourself being friendlier to others, and in turn they'll want to become friends with you. Where do you find that new seed—the seed of possibility that changes misery to happiness, insecurity to confidence, fear to faith, failure to success? It's right where you are, at the very center of your wonderful, magnificent being! You access it by paying attention to your own inner wisdom/intuition/gut feeling/the God of your understanding. Become willing to listen and then take action. Your life will change because *you* change, one new seed at a time!

When I started Al-Anon my self-esteem was shot. I was told to do a daily anonymous act of kindness. I thought, *Okay, even though the rest of my life feels totally out of control, I can do that.* Being secretly helpful became a game, and it was fun! Sneaking around finding anonymous ways to lend a hand placed me fully in the moment and away from my story. I learned that I didn't need to be noticed or thanked to feel good. I started to like who I was becoming! I was planting a new seed of self-worth, one act of kindness at a time.

≈

This week I'll try having at least one ongoing conversation with the God of my understanding, pretending that it hears every word—because it does! I'll write about the experience here.

_____

_____

In what ways have I changed my thinking from negative to positive? How has my life changed because of it?

_____

_____

My thoughts about my spiritual journey are shifting and changing. In this moment, what is God/Spirit/Source to me?

_____

_____

Now it's time to dream! What's one thing that I haven't done that I'd love to do?

_____

_____

Try this: Make a list of 10 attributes that define your Higher Power—truths that you want to *experience* from the God of your understanding. For instance:

- My God is trustworthy; I really can trust that my Higher Power has my back.
- My Higher Power accepts me unconditionally, even when I've blown it and it's hard for me to accept myself.
- My prayers are heard, no matter what they are, how they're spoken, or even if they're just a cry for help in my head.
- I'm never alone; my Higher Power is always with me, no matter what my life looks like.

1. _____

2. _____

3. _____

4. _____

5. _____

6. _____

7. _____

8. _____

9. _____

10. _____

Pay attention to when and how you start to experience evidence that the God of your understanding is showing up in your life in the attributes you've listed. Write about it here.

❧ How the God of My Understanding is Showing Up in My Life ❧

FIVE

BECOME WILLING TO TRUST

Willingness invites action. If you become willing to change a behavior, you'll get opportunities to practice. For instance, if you're willing to become more loving, a person's unkind remark will give you a chance to stay calm instead of lashing out with the need defend or to have the last word. If you're willing to become more prosperous, you'll give a big "Hurray!" for the dime you found lodged in the corner of the couch.

The same is true about becoming willing to trust that the God of your understanding is on your side, that you are loved unconditionally—even on your worst days—and that your Higher Power is right where you are . . . always. When I was eleven I got my first pair of glasses. On the way home from the optometrist's office, I found a whole new world waiting for me! I noticed leaves on the trees where before there were hazy green blobs. There really were planes in the sky leaving those white trails everyone talked about! A new level of awareness and confidence was born that day simply because I literally saw the world through new eyes.

A spiritual awakening is kind of like putting on that first pair of glasses. Before the awakening, your life's purpose is blurry, which may cause you to bump into walls and trip over obstacles in the way, with the spillage generally making a mess of things. You keep stumbling along wondering what you're doing wrong, comparing your life to those who certainly seem to be on the right road, especially in those challenging times when you can't even find the path!

An awareness of a God that's real for you opens your eyes to a relationship with the Divine Essence that is alive and well within you and all around you; you just didn't see it before. You may have struggled with relationships, looking for love, unaware that the most important relationship of all is the one you have with yourself. As your spiritual essence comes into focus, you begin to have an awareness that life is conspiring for your highest good. You will sense it when you're feeling happy and fulfilled, and with a feeling of underlying hope when you're less than happy. Your trust builds.

It's important to remember that you are at choice. Whether you choose to focus on what's wrong or be open to new possibilities, your life will reflect your thinking. If you think life is hard, you get to be right—it will be hard. If you're open to change and become willing to follow new paths, joy and fulfillment await.

Einstein was once asked what he thought the most important question was that a human being needed to answer and he replied, "Is the universe a friendly place?" It's a good question! At the moment of creation, we were given the free will to create and explore each life experience without judgment. With our free will, we co-create life through the power of our thought. If we believe the universe is unfriendly, life becomes a continuation of struggles, we're always bracing ourselves for the next crisis, and we wonder why our back hurts or we can't sleep. If we believe the universe is friendly, we trust that the God of our understanding is in everything that happens. In our most difficult challenges, our faith in a God that is real to us guides us through, and our trust deepens. We learn to accept life's contradictions—difficulty and ease, pain and pleasure, birth and death. Our challenges become an opportunity to learn and be the person we truly want to be.

❧ ❧ ❧

The willingness to change the way that you think about life guides your decisions and your actions. There is power in becoming a place of peace and possibility in every situation. This practice develops an ever-deepening awareness of your spiritual nature. It turns you toward love instead of fear, clarity instead of confusion, acceptance instead of judgment.

Once you begin this practice, you may begin to notice

- the ability to let go of a comment that would have upset you in the past;

- a sense of gratitude at something as simple as taking a shower;

- freedom from a situation that used to trigger you;

- the joy that comes from liking who you see in the mirror.

Welcome to the world of the Beloved One, the God of your understanding! It's *your* world—it always has been. Your true Self . . . your soul . . . your inner wisdom . . . has never been hurt, frightened, angry or victimized. It sits like a vast reservoir of harmony and joy within you. In any moment, an awareness of this great inner love guides you to your most fulfilled life, one tiny step at a time. Slowly, as you consciously shift your focus, your perception and thoughts begin to change, your attitude brightens, and new patterns of behavior take you down a road of joy, abundance, creativity, and self-worth. Is it easy? No. Is it worth it? Absolutely!

It takes as long as it takes to have a spiritual awakening. It took me fifty years, and I'm grateful for every single second of that first fifty years, even the worst days. I see those years with gratitude today because I know that every situation brought me closer to the day when I would discover that God was real. The present moment . . . right now . . . is when you get to consciously choose *your* perspective. There is a reason that in this moment you are reading these words and doing this work. Is something stirring in you now? Pay attention to it! I bet it has to do with seeing the world through new eyes—the spiritual spectacles of possibility. It's your open invitation to live your highest potential, your greatest happiness.

The path is yours to take, knowing each step is blessed. In doing so you are choosing love. You are choosing you.

∼

Do I truly believe that *something in me*—an inner wisdom—knows what to do?

_____

_____

How do I access it, or how *might* I access it? (e.g. in nature, in meditation or prayer, journaling, while I'm gardening, washing the dishes, dancing, thinking about what I'm grateful for.)

_____

_____

Learning to trust that the universe is a friendly place is a process! On a scale of one to ten, with one being no trust at all and ten being very trusting, where am I in my belief that the universe is a friendly place? I'll illustrate with specific examples.

_____

_____

How will fostering a relationship with the God of my understanding influence my trust in a friendly universe?

_____

_____

When have synchronistic moments—when seemingly non-related incidents led to a good result—happened in my life? For instance, I may have moved and then found a new friend. Or perhaps it was the phone call that made a difference in my life, or a struggle that turned out to be a blessing.

Try this: Use this affirmation (or another one of your choice) to move through the next week: "Today I use every opportunity to practice being a place of peace and grace. I *am* peace. I *am* grace." Say it out over and over. Start your day with it, say it silently or aloud in every situation throughout your day, and repeat it again before you sleep at night.

Write your affirmation down and keep it with you in the car, put it on the bathroom mirror, any place that it will remind you of who you truly are. Notice how your reactions to life change.

Begin by writing your affirmation on the following page.

∾ My Affirmation ∾

My affirmation:

How this is changing my life:

∾ Notes ∾

SIX

Understanding Spiritual Laws

Spiritual laws are a gift of the Creator. They go hand in hand with free will, your freedom of choice. Full comprehension of the laws offers you an understanding of why your life is the way it is and an opportunity to head in a new direction, if that's what you choose. You are much more powerful than you may believe yourself to be! The shift in consciousness that occurs when you embrace spiritual laws allows you to take responsibility for *what is,* with the understanding that if your life isn't as joyous as you want it to be, changing your thinking will start to turn that around.

If you have a situation in your life that's less than desirable, don't be discouraged! As you make a conscious decision to change the way you think about that situation, the vibration of your new perspective is noticed and acted upon by that friendly universe that's tuned into you personally. Because the universe is made of the stuff of the Creator, its nature is balance, abundance, orderliness, clarity and expansiveness. It stands ready to bring about circumstances that correspond to your fresh, uplifting thought, as you begin to bring your life back into balance. The process of change takes time, patience, and practice. It begins by understanding how the spiritual laws work.

ᴇꙅ ᴇꙅ ᴇꙅ

The Law of Cause and Effect

"It is done unto you as you believe." What you believe carries a lot of weight! Your beliefs become true for you through the Law of Cause and Effect. Cause is the thought, feeling or belief that you plant in the fertile soil of your mind; it doesn't matter whether it's positive or negative. The thought is acted upon automatically, just as soil automatically grows a plant. The Effect is the resulting experience; it mirrors the thought, feeling or belief that you planted. If you plant anger, you get more reasons to be angry. If you plant victimization, you'll get more situations in which to feel like a victim. The good news is that once you change what you plant (Cause) the result (Effect) will reflect that change.

For example, if you wake up in the morning after not having slept well and you don't feel like going to work, you have a choice. You can brood: *I don't feel good. I'm tired. I don't want to go to work.* That thought—and the feeling energy behind it—becomes the Cause. It is acted upon by the creative process of the Law of Cause and Effect, which works automatically. The result will most likely be a less-than-satisfying day, which is the Effect. As well, your negativity sets into motion a negative tomorrow, as that is the seed you've planted.

Now that you understand this Law, you can choose a different experience! You can inwardly announce: *I want to plant a positive experience, so I intend to have a fine day! Tonight I'll get a good night's sleep, and today I will look for things to be grateful for. I'll spread joy wherever I go! I also know my tomorrows will manifest even more good because that's the seed I'm planting today.*

The co-creative process of Life responds with, "And so it is!"

The Law of Attraction

The Law of Attraction is all about feelings! The feelings you give out, you get back. Your feelings create a vibrational field around you that acts like a magnet, attracting to you people, circumstances and events that are in the same magnetic field. If your vibrational field is optimistic, you will attract people and situations who are relishing the goodness of life. If you are feeling discouraged or pessimistic, you will attract people and circumstances that match your negativity.

For instance, if someone asks you for a favor that will take several hours, be aware of how the prospect feels to you. If you truly want to do the favor, shout out a happy yes! Your act of joyous service to another comes back to you in many positive circumstances. However, if you don't want to do it, it's okay to say no, "Thanks for asking, but I need to say no this time." Let go of the old belief that you have to put everyone else first. Embrace the new! Affirm, "Good for me for taking care of myself and setting a healthy boundary with love!" The important thing is to pay attention to how you *feel* as you make your decision and then follow through, knowing that your feelings about your decision are creative.

Learning to trust the process and the outcome, let the good fortune of others be cause for your own happiness. Be pleased when a co-worker gets a raise, a friend buys a new car, or a stranger wins the lottery. Letting go of envy, you attract pleasing circumstances into your life just as if you'd received the raise or won the lottery. It's not the particular experience that is creative; instead it's how you *feel* about it. Your joy for another attracts the same kind of joy into your life.

The Law of Circulation

As a spiritual being, the same qualities of the Creator are true for you: clarity, peace, abundance, balance, beauty, joy and everything else that radiates positivity. Whatever you want, the Law of Circulation says you must first give it. In order to give it, you must realize that you already *are* it. If you want peace in your life, you first realize that at your core you *are* peace; peace is your nature as a spiritual being. That which you give out, by the Law of Circulation, comes back to you. When you are peaceful, you give out peace, and then more peace returns to you. In a potentially challenging situation, ask yourself, *What would peace do now?* and then do it. That's how it works!

Today, Quantum Physics explains that everything is energy—waves of possibility—until it is observed. Once observed, the waves collapse into particles, and form is created. What you pay attention to—positive or negative—you're observing and causing to collapse into form. If you focus on the negative, more negativity shows up in form—stubbing your toe, a flat tire, an unexpected bill. As soon as you start practicing focusing on what's good in the world, more good starts to show up in everyday life circumstances. Let this understanding guide your decisions when you're considering what to read or watch on television, who to hang out with, how to respond to someone who doesn't agree with you, and how to handle your negativity about your noisy neighbor, going to the dentist or taking out the trash. What do you want to collapse into form, more negativity or more positivity?

Spiritual laws act on your behalf without judgment—they automatically respond to your energy. You are deserving of a beautiful life! The universe really is on your side, forever giving you the opportunity to create more of what makes you happy. Giving and receiving love in your daily life becomes easier when you choose it. The more you choose it, the more it comes back to you, and so it goes. Today, embrace yourself and know that you are loveable and worthwhile. You are the Beloved's magnificent one! Say yes to the goodness and glory of the life that is seeking to make its way to you!

~

In what areas of my life have I already made positive changes?

_____

_____

How did I make those changes? What did I do?

_____

_____

Knowing that I'm a powerful creator, what other parts of my life do I want to change?

_____

_____

Is there anything that has been stopping me? If so, what is it?

_____

_____

What's one thing I can do to get past any obstacles in order to begin moving in a new direction?

_____

_____

What does trusting the God of my understanding have to do with moving forward?

_____

_____

Try this: Make a list of 15 simple things that make you happy and do at least one of them every day. Notice how this bit of self-care changes your attitude and the flow of your daily life.

1. _____

2. _____

3. _____

4. _____

5. _____

6. _____

7. _____

8. _____

9. _____

10. _____

11. _____

12. _____

13. _____

14. _____

15. _____

∽ How Self-Care is Affecting My Life ∽

SEVEN

PEELING THE ONION SOMETIMES MAKES YOU CRY

Before I knew God was real and before I understood spiritual laws, I thought life just happened. I could hope for the best, but I had no idea that my attitude was creative. I felt sorry for myself when things didn't go my way, looking for people to commiserate with, "Ain't it awful?" Of course, my self-pity was also creative. Even though I didn't want that situation in my life, I sure paid a lot of attention to it! Now I know that when I pay a lot of attention to the negativity in my life, I get more negativity. It's definitely a learning process!

It's not coincidental that I was in Al-Anon at the time of my awakening, that moment when I knew the God of my understanding was real. As my eyes were opened to the greatest Love of all, my mind was opened to the power of my creative thinking. Around that time my sponsor started taking me to the local new thought church she attended, and I began to hear a lot about *change your thinking; change your life.* Spiritual laws were explained and I began to appreciate the power of my very creative mind. If I kept an optimistic outlook, found the good in everything, my life would improve in every area—relationships, money, health, jobs, self-esteem—the works!

I started doing the work of incorporating positive thinking into my life, and in many cases I could see and feel the positive results! At the same time, my ego rebelled against all that optimism—didn't I know that the world was a scary place? I had to consciously try to keep that old ego-thinking in check. Some of my previous beliefs were tested—were they still true today? The process of peeling back the layers of the Jane-onion to discover who I was today was now in full swing! I was beginning to understand the reality of what it meant to be a spiritual being having a human experience. As a spiritual being I was perfect, but as a human being I was perfectly imperfect! To me, my job was to accept myself in all of my human messiness. Peeling back those onion layers was essential, as I discovered more of who I was underneath each layer. In the process I ran into a few road blocks.

There was one big problem with the whole *change your thinking, change your life* thing. What was I supposed to do when big challenges hit and I was terrified? It wasn't at all helpful for people to say, "Stay positive! Don't be afraid; it will all work out." How did *they* know? And how does one 'not be afraid'? What about when I lay in bed at night worried about a loved one? How do I erase worry? Then there were the times when my ego was screaming, "Don't even try that new class, job, friendship, adventure—it won't work; you're not qualified; they're going to find out you're not as good as you pretend to be!" How was I supposed to move past my fear, the worry that kept me up at night, and the negative voice of my ego? Lurking under the layers of my onion were panic, judgment, guilt, and a whole slew of other negative feelings ready to jump out and squash my new positive attitude. I was quickly learning that peeling away the onion layers sometimes made me cry.

Then one day I sensed the presence of the Beloved One, which spoke to me through a feeling . . . a thought . . . a message brought to me from deep within me via the wisdom of my soul. It said, *Bring your negative emotions to me. Let me hold you while you feel them. None of your feelings are wrong—they're part of your human experience. They're part of you, and you are my cherished one. I love all of you, including your negative feelings. After a while you will learn to accept those feelings and then they won't frighten you anymore. Bring them to me, and in the safety of my embrace, discover what they have to teach you.* So that's what I did.

I sat on my couch, a box of tissues handy because I was already weeping with the enormity of the Beloved's message—imagine feeling so loved that I became willing to look at the emotions that gripped me with terror! Even though I was scared, I did my best to relax into the loving energy of the One that adored me. I soon began to feel the tender movement of the Beloved's energy, softly wrapping itself around me like a gentle breeze on a summer's night whispering, *You're safe. You are my cherished one. You are meant to be happy. You are perfect, just as you are. Feel your feelings. They are part of you, and I love you.*

Soon fear bubbled up to the surface, creating a knot in my stomach. The Beloved whispered, *Good, here is fear. Ask it to teach you what you need to know.*

Silently, I asked, *Fear, what is it you want to show me? What do I need to know?*

Fear answered through images in my mind, memories of all the times I let fear stop me from saying what needed to be said or doing what needed to be done. There were so many! I cried as I saw them, remembering the shame and guilt, the anger and resentment toward others and especially toward myself. Then there were visions of the many instances when, acting out of fear, I did or said things that caused pain to myself or someone else. As one scene after another came up, each triggered memories and emotions I'd tried to push away because I didn't want to deal with them. At the same time I could feel the energy of the Beloved surrounding me, gently easing my tendency to halt the process. It silently encouraged me to stay the course. I knew I needed to let fear speak through all those flashbacks and most importantly, I needed to notice my response to them. I could almost hear the Beloved say, *Fear's message is essential; pay attention. It's part of you; learn from it.*

Finally, after what seemed like hours, but in truth was about sixty minutes, came a big "Aha!" moment. I started to become aware of tendencies that repeated themselves, patterns of fear-based reactions that had controlled my life. When something scary happened I reacted in a certain way, which soon became a habit—I kept reacting in the same way! Although the situations changed, my response to them pretty much stayed the same. It was like looking at someone else's life on a movie screen—I could now see what I had been doing to myself! I began to notice to what extent those old fears were still playing themselves out in my life today; my reactions were still the same, hanging on out of habit.

So this is what fear wanted to teach me, that as a human being, I'm a creature of habit! Once I started reacting with fear, fear gathered steam like a locomotive heading down the side of a mountain, each new scary experience adding to the personal fear-bag that I carried around. I also knew that I was the owner of my fear, and therefore I could drop the bag and let go of those old fearful patterns. I realized that every moment of my life I'm either living more fully or withdrawing into less. I can work with life circumstances or struggle against them. I can challenge my fears or believe them. I can expand my point of view or try to protect it. I can believe in myself or find myself lacking. I can hold onto my habits or set myself free.

It's a process! I'm more courageous now than I used to be. Every time I set a boundary, say what I need or stand up for what's important to me, an old habit is broken and my courage grows. Even if my stomach is doing flip flops as I take that next step, I feel brave! I'm my own hero! I don't even have to do it well; I just need to do it. Courage helps me awaken to the unexpected strength that I've had all along.

My feelings are part of me, all of them. They invite me to see myself through the eyes of awareness—what is true today. With self-understanding, self-acceptance and self-compassion, I do my best to lean into my feelings to ask, *What is asking for attention?* or, *What is asking for acceptance?* or, *What do I need to know?* staying open to what the emotion is teaching me. I'm learning to be a willing and grateful student. My feelings are my teachers when I allow myself to be teachable. The God that adores me holds and guides me through the lesson, bit by bit peeling away the layers of the onion that is me. It isn't easy, and it often makes me cry, but it is worth it because *I'm* worth it. So are you. So are we all. We're all meant to be happy, and part of that happiness is accepting all parts of ourselves.

∾

I'm on a path of understanding who I am . . . all of me. Am I willing to look at my negative feelings as a normal and natural part of me?

_____

_____

Am I willing to see my negative feelings as my teachers?

_____

_____

How have I hidden from my feelings in the past?

_____

_____

What has been the result?

_____

_____

Am I willing to choose a negative emotion and ask it to teach me what I need to know?

_____

_____

Try this:

Using the drawing on the next page or creating your own, draw a simple picture of an onion.

✧ Color a bright yellow star at the center of the onion, symbolic of the shining light that is *you*.

✧ Take a few moments to contemplate where you are in the process of peeling away the layers of the onion to discover that bright light within you.

◆ Are you at the beginning, the outside of the onion, still thinking about peeling back the first layer?

◆ Have you peeled back one or two layers, getting the process started?

◆ Draw an arrow to the place on the onion that represents where you are on your journey of self-discovery today.

▹ Label it "I am here," and date it.

▹ As you peel back a layer, moving toward the center of the onion, draw and date a new arrow to show your progress.

See how far you've come!

~ My Onion ~

EIGHT

Choosing Happiness

The love of God is who you are. The peace of God is your nature. Love, peace, joy and wisdom are built into your divine DNA. When I first realized this I asked the Beloved, *If this is true, then why is my life such a mess sometimes?* Then my own answers came bubbling up from the wisdom of my soul: It's true that spiritually I'm absolutely perfect. However, I'm living a human life with the thoughts, feelings and experiences that go with it, and the drama of that human life can be very intoxicating!

Before I knew God was real I got caught up in the whirlwind of what was around me, unaware that beneath the surface there was a vast reservoir of peace. It took dedicated practice to change my perspective, understanding that in every single human experience I was at choice as to how to see it and how to move through it. That's one reason that I wrote this workbook. My hope is that it will help you to realize the same.

The God of your understanding is your personal guide as you accept your human life experiences without making them wrong—or making *you* wrong. At the same time it moves you toward the life you dream about, the one filled with meaning and happiness. Your God is there even when you can't sense its presence. It's always been there and always will be. Look back at your life with all its ups and downs. You weren't alone. You've never been alone. Think of the times when you were frightened as a child and somehow you made it through.

The greatest Love of all gave you the tenacity, endurance, and the will to go on; you just may not have recognized it. In small ways it offered the young, frightened you avenues for hope, perhaps in the imaginative play with a favorite toy or the creativity of finding shapes in the clouds. In reality, the Beloved *was* the toy. It *was* the clouds. It was an inner comfort when you couldn't find comfort in the outside world. It gave you the courage to move through your fear when you didn't think you could do it. Today, the Beloved still offers gentle direction. It continues to help you notice the beauty of what's around you, and especially the beauty of who you are. It offers you the hope that you really can move past any emotional pain to find the serenity you intuitively know exists.

In allowing yourself to be guided to your greatest happiness, you will be called upon to let go of old ways of thinking and old behaviors that are holding you back. How do you take the first step? How can you begin to embrace something as elusive as inner peace when you may have been steeped in sadness, blame and regret?

Generally, there are three basic steps, each offered by the patient and wise guidance of your soul—your own inner wisdom.

The first step is to become *aware* of what drives your behavior, especially your negative behavior. Is it poor self-esteem, addictive behaviors, despondency over losing a job or relationship, financial challenges, illness, childhood abuse or any other conditions which interfere with being as happy as you want to be? Becoming aware offers the opportunity to notice what you think about, why you don't do the things you really want to do, and why you sometimes feel so sad, along with the invitation to be done with the pain. When you want to heal more than anything in the world, you are at a crossroad in your life. You get to choose whether to be the victim of your story or the hero of your story. In the process you open the door to your Higher Power, the one that stands ready to lead you to physical, mental, emotional and spiritual health. You don't have to know how it's going to happen; you just need to believe that it *can* happen. You will begin to write a new chapter in the story of your life, one of transformation, as you center on faith and possibility instead of the way your life used to be.

The second step is to become *willing* to change. Setting the intention to lay down past beliefs and behaviors sometimes stops people as they ask, "As much as I want my life to change, if I let go of who I've been, who will I become? If I let go of anger, resentment and self-blame, what will be left of me? If I can no longer control those around me, what will happen to my relationships?"

When I was in Al-Anon I asked that question often. If I let go of my old thinking, what would replace it? I sometimes thought I'd turn into Swiss cheese, full of holes where my old victimization used to hang out! Even though my life wasn't working, at least it had been familiar. Becoming willing to change is a powerful step forward, one that's essential to taking command of the one thing that you can control—you.

The unknown road to peace is often so scary that sometimes people unconsciously sabotage their journey with old behaviors, just as they reach the threshold of success. I've done it! I learned to treat myself gently in the process of change. Slowly I discovered that with faith and a willingness to keep at it, I could replace who I'd been with who I was born to be. As I consciously practiced letting go of resentment, my natural state of acceptance stood ready to take its place. As I let go of self-judgment, I learned to like myself, even when I made big mistakes. There was a whole new side of me just waiting to emerge, and it's someone I liked!

The third step in being guided to your greatest happiness is to *accept* every situation as an opportunity for growth, brought to you by a gracious universe in order for you to practice being who you want to be. This is especially true for situations you tend to see as negative. Ask yourself, "If this situation is in my life anyway, why not look at it as a chance to be who I want to be instead of a reason to feel angry? How will I know inner peace if I don't have an opportunity to practice being peaceful?"

In every circumstance, you can choose where to put your focus. Your focal point can be on harmony, love and acceptance, guided by the wisdom of your soul, or you can let judgment run rampant and center your attention on frustration, bitterness and resentment, which are ego-based and take you right back to being the victim of your story. Always, no matter what the situation, your perception of it is up to you—it's your free will. Your focus directs your attitude, and your attitude guides your actions—the way you want your story to play itself out. It begins with the conscious decision to be guided by what's important to you.

Embracing the love of a God that adores you is a big step. In order to truly accept and learn from every circumstance, it starts with believing that the God of your understanding is inherently good and that life is on your side. In any moment you can choose to say, "My life, in this very instant, is a gift from the Beloved One who cherishes me. I'm grateful for everything in my life right now, including this experience, even though I wouldn't have chosen it. Somehow, good is going to come from it." The good that comes from it is often your decision to practice a new way of being, with a different attitude, a growing faith and an increasing level of self-worth.

Remember, you are a powerful creator. The universe pays attention to your thoughts and actions, standing ready to create a life that's gloriously happy, meant just for you! It takes strength to make the changes that head your new life in the direction that you want to travel. You have what it takes—you are strong, capable, intelligent, and brave. You deserve the best! The universe stands ready to co-create your new life with you, conspiring for your success.

≈

Here I'll describe a time when I was really frightened.

_____

_____

What did I learn about myself as I moved through it?

_____

_____

When I look back at it now, where was the God of my understanding in all of it?

_____

_____

Knowing that I'm a powerful creator, what's one next step I'm willing to take toward living the gloriously happy life I'm meant to live?

_____

_____

What's one negative behavior that I'm willing to release? (e.g. judgment, procrastination, complaining)

_____

_____

What might that negativity be replaced with? (e.g. acceptance, taking responsibility, optimism)

_____

_____

Try this: Begin looking for new things to be grateful for, from the fact that you have food to put in your stomach to toothpaste to brush your teeth. How long has it been since you told your deodorant you were grateful for it? Do it! Everything counts!

Find or draw pictures to create a collage below of some of the simple things you're grateful for today.

> ∼ I'm Grateful! ∼

≈ Notes ≈

NINE

DIVINE DISCONTENT

Have you ever been in a job, relationship, or a pattern of behavior that used to bring you pleasure but is no longer satisfying? Nothing has changed except *you*—now you're bored, antsy, resentful and envious of others. This is actually a good thing! It's called divine discontent and it's your call to step into change. Divine discontent is different than being annoyed or frustrated. Annoyance comes from wanting someone else to change so that you will feel better. If they straighten up their act, if that situation changes, life will be a lot easier! Divine discontent is *your* part, *your* responsibility, the invitation for *you* to make a change.

This divine discontent happens when something new beckons and you are hesitating. You're attempting to stay with what's familiar, trying to find satisfaction in a world that's now too small for you. You want to stay there because it's what you know, and yet it's no longer serving you like it used to. It's like a baby bird in an egg. First the egg is comforting, and then as the bird grows it starts to feel cramped. The bird wishes it had a bigger egg. However, the bird's next step is to start pecking its way out of that small, cramped egg. Then the egg cracks open and the bird finds a new, expansive world outside. The process begins when the baby bird takes action.

Divine discontent is an indication that it's time for you to break out of some area of your life. Sometimes you know right away what the discontent is about and what you need to do about it. More often, the discontent settles in but you can't put your finger on it; it's difficult to figure out what's up. Months may go by and then all of a sudden there's an Aha! moment when you know what you need to do. Then it's up to you.

Divine discontent is *for* you and not against you, even though it doesn't feel good at all. The discontent has to be uncomfortable enough to get your attention. It won't leave you alone because you're supposed to do something about it. The process is ultimately about you awakening to your own potential; you alone are the one that has to do the changing in order to live up to that potential. The discomfort generally comes right before it's time for a big shift or next step. It's Life nudging you forward.

I felt divine discontent before I finally ended my marriage. I was like the baby bird in the egg, wishing I had a bigger egg . . . struggling with the life I had once chosen . . . filled with guilt for even thinking about leaving . . . telling myself I could make it work. But something more was calling me, and the egg felt tighter and tighter. Needing to break out, I was terrified to leave! I'd been married since I was twenty-one; I had no idea how not to be married. And what about all those people who would be hurt and disappointed if I left? For a people-pleaser, the thought of leaving was extraordinary difficult, and yet divine discontent kept knocking at my door. Something was urging me forward. I could no longer settle for life as it had been before.

It was during this time that I discovered that God was real. The only way I could walk through my fear was by focusing on the Beloved. I learned that I could trust it and that I was worthy of the brand new life that was waiting for me, even though I had no idea what that was. So I listened, and I followed divine direction. I began to learn that there was much more to me than I thought—I was more capable than I realized, and I was cautiously curious about what was ahead. So one tiny step at a time—just like the little bird pecking out of the egg—I moved forward. Held in grace, I somehow knew what to do and how to do it. Listening to divine direction, I knew what to say, when to say it, and when to say nothing. A new faith in *me* started to grow. The moment I moved into my townhouse, living on my own, I recognized that something magical was happening, and I was filled with the excitement of it!

A year later divine discontent once again showed up on my doorstep; it was time to leave my twenty-year teaching career. Before that my intention was to make teaching my lifelong profession, at least another ten years before I'd even consider retiring. At the time, I wasn't even old enough to collect retirement, but there was divine discontent. My ego shouted, "How do you think you're going to live? Where do you think the money will come from?" But this time the recent experience of trusting enough to leave my marriage was still fresh in my mind. During that experience my faith had grown by leaps and bounds, and I knew that I could do this, too. Without another job, or even any idea what direction to take, I submitted my resignation. When people asked me why I was resigning I'd say, "I'm following a dream," to which they'd ask, "What dream?" My answer was simply, "I don't know." And yet something inside me did know, so I followed each tiny step as it was revealed to me. Of course Life was leading me toward becoming a minister, but that wasn't even in my wildest imagination at that time. I just knew that somehow—even though it was really scary—it was safe for me to move ahead. With every step, my faith continued to grow.

✑ ✑ ✑

You'll find that as you begin to follow your inner guidance, the universe will begin to create a space for your success. Doors will open on your behalf. That doesn't mean it's easy—lots of it is really hard. What it does mean is that it's worth it. You will get to practice walking through your fear, trusting your gut instinct, learning that you are smarter and more tenacious than you ever knew. In the process you'll strengthen yourself mentally, emotionally and spiritually—all necessary to live your new life. You'll discover what's important to you and you'll become willing to stand up for it. Every day you'll practice being the person you want to be, the person you were meant to be.

Just as sure as you let divine discontent propel you forward, you can bet that others will notice the difference in you. Some will rejoice for you! For others, the change will be uncomfortable because you're not playing the role you've always played, the one that's predictable . . . the one that makes them feel okay. With divine discontent comes the willingness to let go of being who others want you to be. Sometimes it means letting go of the people and situations that are no longer in your best interest. Somehow, behind the fears and doubts of letting go, you'll realize that it's time to put *you* first.

Divine discontent at work, the new you may find an increasing need to make changes in your daily life. Your very human mind might argue, *Do I just get rid of my prized collections after I had so much fun accumulating them all these years? Why is it that suddenly they feel like clutter in my life?*

Your tastes may begin to change, too. *Why am I'm no longer interested in the same books or TV shows I used to watch? Why is that hobby not as exciting as it used to be?*

Then there are those old friends, *Am I supposed to leave them behind? And yet I continually find myself making excuses instead of being available when they call. What is this? Something in me is certainly changing, and I don't know what to do about it!*

Feeling a pull away from the familiar can be scary, and at the same time the stirring within you compels you to do it. Divine discontent is one of Life's great blessings, a natural part of spiritual awakening. It urges you to move in a new direction that requires faith and courage, for there is more for you to know, do and be. It's the next step in your spiritual journey. Letting go is essential—if you try to bring along everyone and everything from your past, you won't make room for the new. With your growing faith, you will be given the courage to make changes when you are called to do so. In your courage, you will say yes to a greater life than you ever imagined. In saying yes to your life, you enjoy the privilege of owning your happiness, which is pure freedom!

Remember that baby bird I mentioned earlier? We can learn from her. If divine discontent is knocking at the door of your heart right now, ask yourself, "Have I settled for a life that feels cramped? If so, what's stopping me from breaking out and moving forward: fear, procrastination, habit, denial?" Trust that you're okay, and then take tiny steps. Say yes instead of no. Trust your gut instinct. Don't settle. You're not too old, too unhealthy, too broke or too wounded to start. Today's a good day to begin.

~

What is one small step I can take this week to begin cracking the shell?

_____

_____

Which five things do I value most in my life today, knowing they may be different than what I used to value? Why do I value them?

1. _____

2. _____

3. _____

4. _____

5. _____

In what areas do I feel a twinge of divine discontent, a need for change? How is the discontent showing up?

1. _____

2. _____

3. _____

4. _____

5. _____

Do I truly believe that I'm capable of changing my life?

_____

_____

Am I willing to own the truth that I'm worthy of something much better?

_____

_____

Where is the God of my understanding in all of this?

_____

_____

Try this: Choose one area that you want to change. Begin to celebrate each small step forward! Write about it here:

~ Celebrating Change – One Small Step at a Time ~

❧ Notes ❧

TEN

GROWING YOUR FAITH

At every given moment you're at choice. What you think about any situation moves you toward success and happiness or failure and dissatisfaction. When you choose to look for the good you tap into your spiritual essence—the beauty of who you truly are. In the process you will start to feel your faith growing; there's an expectation that whatever the circumstance, somehow you'll know what to do with it, and things will work out. You don't need to figure out or control how it will happen—you only know that it will. You take the time to listen . . . really listen . . . to the wisdom that is within you. Only then do you act, taking your cue from the spiritual voice that speaks only of truth and possibility.

How you sense that voice—the wisdom of your soul—is unique to you. For me, it's not really a voice; I don't 'hear' it; it's more of a feeling . . . an unexpected thought . . . a knowing. It's often the first positive thought that comes up once I've become quiet enough to pay attention. Sometimes it's a brand new idea. It regularly reminds me to look for what's right instead of what's wrong. Looking for what's right opens up a whole mountain of possibilities that would have remained unavailable had I not created the space for them to show up. It takes practice. Whenever an old habitual negative thought enters my mind, I practice replacing it with an optimistic one, or I find something to be grateful for. My inner cheerleader walks me through every step; my job is to pay attention and act on the wisdom that it provides.

As your increasing faith turns you toward the God of your understanding, you will find that your old stuff will surface—memories you'd just as soon forget. No worries! Those old thoughts, beliefs and memories come up so that you can take a fresh look at them. Now that you're spiritually stronger you see them through your new eyes of faith. It may be time to gently start letting them go. You are accepted without condition by a God that adores you, just as you are, and that counts for everything in your past, too. When the shameful memories come up, you are at a moment of creative choice: Will you drag that old shame into your life today? You now know that the feeling of shame is creative and attracts more reasons to feel ashamed, which gives you something to think about. Take time to listen to what shame has to teach you. Allow yourself to be teachable. As you learn to value the lessons that shame provides, you will know how to replace shame with self-acceptance, self-understanding, self-compassion and self-for-giveness. The God of your understanding adored you when the shame was created, and it cherishes you now as you reflect on it. What will you choose?

As you practice you will find that you have developed a larger container for receiving the good you want in life because you're beginning to understand that you are *worthy* of that good. You *deserve* that good.

When you embrace the power of your own creative nature, your life will change as it reflects each new decision. In the Try This section on page 91 of this chapter, you'll find an activity called "Evidence of Change" in which you are asked write down every tiny bit of evidence that things are changing on your behalf. This builds your faith muscle! By noticing the good that comes into your life, as well as the positive changes in the way you see yourself, you are planting trust and faith in the fertile soil of your mind—the Law of Cause and Effect in action. Your new perceptions will begin to manifest new, positive results.

Here's how the Evidence of Change works: Write down thoughts, situations and events that are evidence of change in your life. For instance, if you've been looking for a new friend and have the idea to take a class at a local college, go for it! That brand new idea may hold the key to a new friendship—perhaps someone you'll meet in class or even in the parking lot, or it will lead to the next class in which friendship is waiting for you. Your excitement initiates the Law of Attraction; others who are also excited about the classes and the possibility of meeting new friends will be attracted to you because you're on the same vibrational level. Your friendliness sets the Law of Circulation into motion—when you are friendly, you call friends to you.

If you want a healthy and energetic body and you don't find a parking place close to your destination, forcing you to walk, good! No more grumbling because you didn't get the parking space you wanted. Every step you take (literally!) says yes to a healthy and energetic body. Write it down with gratitude!

If you're looking for more prosperity in your life and your favorite cereal is on sale or your friend picks up the tab for coffee, write it down! Your gratitude about money is contagious, and the universe will bring more reasons to feel grateful.

Also note the changes in your relationship with yourself and in your relationship with the God of your understanding. This is the evidence that your faith is increasing. As your awareness of spiritual laws grows, so will your faith. Because you are endeavoring to *be* peace, love, and joy, you will find yourself turning toward your inner wisdom for answers and next steps. Trusting that all is well and you are okay, your personal relationship with the God of your understanding will deepen and grow. Where and how do you notice the changes? Write them down!

As you lean into Divine Love, realize how precious you really are, and everything will begin to take care of itself; you no longer have to be in charge of the world! Understand that the universe co-creates with you through the spiritual laws. They create on your behalf. When you appreciate and accept that you are deserving of a beautiful life, the universe will gladly give it to you. Giving and receiving love to yourself and others becomes easier because you choose it. The more you choose it, the more it comes to you, and so it goes.

Today, embrace yourself and know that you are worthwhile. You are the Beloved's magnificent one. Say *yes* to the goodness and glory of life that is seeking to make its way to you!

∽

In what ways have I become kinder, more generous or more good-humored?

_____

_____

In what ways have I quit being so controlling with others?

_____

_____

In what areas am I willing to ask the God of my understanding for help in order to be the person I want to be?

_____

_____

Being held in Divine Guidance and Love this very moment, what gifts have the changes in the last few years brought to me?

_____

_____

Try this: Turn to page 91 and get started on the Evidence of Change section. Don't go to sleep until you've thought back on the day to see the good in it, including the good in *you!* Then write it down.

∼ Today this is ME! ∼

As I begin to get a glimpse of the way the God of my understanding sees me, I'll draw or find photos that represent what my full potential might look like/feel like. It may look like the sun shining through the trees, an ocean sunrise, a lantern in the darkness, a collage of bright colors—anything goes!

∼ What I Believe Could Be Possible ∼

Today I believe the following could be possible about the God of my understanding:

1. _____

   _____

2. _____

   _____

3. _____

   _____

Today I believe the following could be possible about *me*:

1. _____
   _____

2. _____
   _____

3. _____
   _____

Today I believe the following could be possible about my *life:*

1. _____

_____

2. _____

_____

3. _____

_____

Hurray, you're on your way!
With love,
   – *Jane*

❧ Evidence of Change ❧

On these pages I will keep a log of thoughts, situations and events that are evidence of change in my life, such as:

- reasons to feel grateful
- positive thoughts that are replacing old negativity
- kindness that has been shown to me or that I have shown to others
- my willingness to step out of my comfort zone to try something new
- seeing the God of my understanding at work in my life
- a growing ability to sense my own inner wisdom
- evidence that my faith is growing
- indications that I am beginning to recognize and appreciate my own self-worth

Sharing What's Been Revealed to You

Using this personal workbook, *How to Build a Relationship with the God of Your Understanding: Start Where You Are*, is a great opportunity to meet with friends or others of like mind, either online or in group settings. Included here are some guidelines which will help ensure the success of each gathering.

Timing

Whether you're meeting weekly, every other week, or monthly my suggestion would be to have each participant do the work on their own, and then have the group come together for discussion. Make a group decision as to:

- Where the meetings will be held
- How often to meet
- The length of time for each meeting

Because every spiritual journey takes time to unfold, I encourage you to allow plenty of time; don't hurry the process. This offers each person an opportunity to be with the insights that come to them and notice the resulting changes in their daily lives. They will then bring their stories, revelations, and questions to the group.

You will recognize yourselves in each other's journeys. Together, from a place of openness and complete acceptance, you will become a support system for each other.

Guidelines for Sharing

It's important that everyone in the group feels safe. This encourages sharing that is open, honest and authentic. Following these guidelines helps set up a format for success.

As discussion begins, become centered in love and compassion. Be aware of the precious gift given when someone has the courage to share him/herself. Make the space for listening when other people are speaking without categorizing what you are hearing as positive or negative.

Confidentiality

- What is said in the group stays in the group.

- If the group is large, there may be times when small groups of 2-4 people break out of the larger group to share. If so, what is said in the small break-out groups stays within that group. When you come back together to share with the whole group, speak of your insights only instead of the revelation of someone else in the small group.

Respectful Listening

- Speak about your own feelings and experiences and not about what someone else has shared as their feelings or experiences.

- Actively listen while another person is speaking and then refrain from commenting or giving advice—no 'fixing.'

- Once a person has shared, the response of the others in the group is, "Thank you," before the next person speaks. This helps keep the tendency to make a comment (which pulls the attention back to the person making the comment) or 'fixing' at bay.

- Respect the rights of others and share one time only within each speaking opportunity. If you later remember something wonderful you intended to mention, wait until everyone else has had their turn.

- Be sensitive to the amount of time you spend in sharing. If communication is easy for you, hold back when needed in order to allow time for others. If sharing is more difficult for you, this is an opportunity to practice speaking up from your perspective.

As a Member of the Group

Remember this is a sacred journey, one in which your participation is essential to the group and to your own personal journey. You will walk alongside the others in your group, honoring every step taken.

Whatever your process looks like, your journey is perfect, just as it is. Bring yourself wholly to your particular experience and to the experience of the group. You are worth your caring attention!

Facilitator

If you've never facilitated before: This workbook offers an opportunity for potential new facilitators to step into the role of facilitator. There's nothing you need to 'teach;' instead you are there to guide the discussion. The Facilitator Guides for Each Chapter"that begin on the following pages were written with you in mind. Gather together your friends, book study group, 12-step pals, or anyone else of like mind and move through this workbook together! You'll find that your role as facilitator enriches your life as you discover that you're much more capable than you thought yourself to be.

If there isn't a designated facilitator: If the group doesn't have a facilitator, one can be chosen within the group or the facilitator position can rotate—a different person each week or each month. If a participant is really uncomfortable with taking on the role of facilitator, they can opt out; this is a judgment-free zone.

ᴇᴏ ᴇᴏ ᴇᴏ

The facilitator creates a safe space, enabling people to relax into their personal relationship with the God of their understanding. It's done by being warm, attentive, organized and as confident as possible in their role as facilitator.

As the facilitator, take time to get yourself centered before the group meets in order to bring the best of who you are to the time you spend together.

Go over these Guidelines for Sharing with your group at the beginning of each chapter as a gentle reminder to the group.

Facilitator Guides for Each Chapter

Step-by-step suggestions for the facilitator

Hello Facilitator Friend.

I've endeavored to make the facilitator guides as easy to follow as possible so that every facilitator is successful, even if you've never led a group before. Under each chapter you will find suggestions as to how to go through that chapter. When you see an italicized section preceded by **Say** or **Ask**, this is your signal that the following material can be read aloud to begin the discussion.

Please use the facilitator guides as *guides.* Pick and choose what works best for you, and let the experience be fluid. The sharing of your personal experiences with the group is invaluable; your openness and honesty sets the tone for others to do the same.

First Meeting Welcome and Introductions:

Before beginning:

Make sure everyone knows where the restrooms are and when you will be taking a break. Ask if there are any other logistical questions to make sure everyone is comfortable.

Say: Welcome to "Building a Relationship with the God of Your Understanding: Start Where You Are."

This group is designed to be a place so safe that you can let down your defenses and relax into your personal relationship with the God of your understanding—your Higher Power. We're all walking the journey together, opening our minds and hearts to include God, whatever we call Him/Her/It.

Say: While our experiences are unique to each of us, we'll also see similarities with others as they share their insights and revelations. Our readiness to be open and honest is the gift we bring to this class. We really do learn from each other!

✓*TIP*

- As the role model, you begin. Others will take their cue from you.
- The opening question helps participants get to know each other. They will find that there are lots of similarities within the group.
- The opening question may also offer one or two of those wonderful, "Aha! I hadn't thought about that; the same is true for me, too!" moments. This helps others realize they aren't alone in their thoughts, feelings and experiences.

Ask: Please introduce yourself and answer the question: What would you like to get out of this group—what do you want to take away from it?

Ask: Are there any questions before we get started?

CHAPTER ONE

Jane's Story: From Atheist to Minister

✓ *TIP*

- If the group is large, ask people to limit their sharing to 2-3 minutes to leave time for others to share.
- If people are hesitant to begin, be ready to offer your own story to get things started.

Whole group

Ask: After reading Jane's story, who would be willing to share a bit of their own story? When did you have an experience of the God of your understanding, an indication that there really is a Higher Power?

* Choose one or two of the questions at the end of Chapter One (p.12-14) for participants to share in small groups.

Small group timing guidelines: Generally, 5 minutes per person per question provides enough time for discussion. Small groups of 2-4 people work well. When you have more time, choose groups of 3 or 4. If you're running short on time, dyads (2 people) can meet.

- Two people, one question (10 min. for the small group discussion)
- Three people, one question (15 min.)
- Four people, one question (20 min.)
- Two people, two questions (20 min.)
- Three people, two questions (30 min.)
- Four people, two questions (40 min.)

Small group discussion (2-4 people)

Once you've decided on the number of people for each group, ask the participants to get into groups to share their answers to the question(s).

Sᴀʏ: Remember that everything said in your small group is confidential. Also remember that there is no 'fixing.' Please don't offer well-meant suggestions.

* (Depending upon the group size and whether you chose one or two questions choose the appropriate amount of time for sharing between 10-40 minutes.)

Sᴀʏ: *You have* _____ (10-40) minutes.* Kindly make sure that those who speak up easily make time for quieter folks to speak. If you are one who tends to stay quiet, use this time to stretch out of your comfort zone and let your thoughts be heard.

Sᴀʏ: I will let you know when there are 5 minutes left. Are there any questions?

✓ *TIP*

- As the facilitator, if you are in a group, watch the time and be ready to leave your small group long enough to let the other groups know there are five minutes left for small group sharing.

Aꜱᴋ: Are there any questions?

Whole group discussion

If time, ask everyone to share one insight that came up for them in their small group discussion, reminding everyone to bring up their thoughts only, not what someone else said.

- If time is limited, ask for 2-3 volunteers to share.
- If time is extremely limited, this part can be omitted.

Whole group

Say: Now it's time to take a look at the Try This section on page 15.

Ask: Who will share what your Higher Power feels like today, or what you want your Higher Power to feel like? Jane gave some possible examples: the feeling of walking on the beach, your pet's fur, waking up after a good night's sleep, holding hands with someone who cares about you.

✧   Have volunteers share.

Closing

Ask each person to say one thing they're grateful for today.

As the facilitator, you go first to set the example.

Say: One thing I'm grateful for is _____.

CHAPTER TWO

Religion or Spirituality? Make a Fresh Start

Whole group

Say: Many of our views are based on our foundations—all the stuff that sits in our minds as memories. Even if we're not conscious of it, the things we've been told, and what we've seen and heard, have influenced us.

Say: In this chapter we look at how the religious beliefs of our childhood—our religious foundation—may have influenced our thoughts about God, ourselves and the world.

Ask: After reading this chapter about religion and spirituality, what impact did your religion of origin have on you as a child?

Ask: If you weren't raised in a particular religion, what did you hear about religion/God and how did it impact you?

✓ *TIP*

- If the group is large, ask people to limit their sharing to 2-3 min. in order to leave time for others to share.
- If you're running short on time: **Say:** "Let's hear from two more people," to let everyone know the discussion is coming to a close.
- If people are hesitant to begin, be ready with your own story to get things started.

---

* Choose one or two of the questions at the end of Chapter Two (p.19-20) for participants to share in small groups; . . . OR

Because everyone's childhood exposure to religion is unique, you may want to have each participant choose one or two of the questions that are most relevant to *them* to share in the small group setting.

Small group discussion (2-4 people)

Ask the participants to get into groups of 2-4 to share their answers to the question(s), either the ones you've chosen or the ones they chose for themselves.

Say: Remember that everything said in your small group is confidential. Also remember that there is no 'fixing.' Please don't offer well-meant suggestions.

* (Depending upon the group size and whether you chose one or two questions, choose the appropriate amount of time for sharing between 10-40 minutes.)

Say: You have* _____ (10-40) minutes. Kindly make sure that those who speak up easily make time for those who tend to be quieter. If you are one who tends to stay quiet, use this time to stretch a bit out of your comfort zone and let your thoughts be heard.

I will let you know when there are 5 minutes left. Are there any questions?

Whole group discussion

If time, ask everyone to share one thing that came up for them in the small group discussion, reminding everyone to comment on their thoughts only, not what someone else said.

- If time is limited, ask for 2-3 volunteers to share.
- If time is extremely limited, this part can be omitted.

Whole group

SAY: Now it's time to take a look at the Try This section on page 21.

ASK: What helps you sense the presence of a Higher Power—being in nature, the company of friends or those who inspire you, reading spiritual material, being in a group like this, feeling grateful, enjoying your favorite activities or hobbies?

- If time, have everyone share one thing, giving others ideas they may not have considered.
- If less time, have volunteers share.

Closing

Have each person share one thing they're grateful for about how they sense the God of their understanding. Examples might be:

- I'm grateful to feel the God of my understanding in nature;
- I'm grateful to sense the God of my understanding when I play my guitar.

CHAPTER THREE

What Are You Listening To: Ego or Your Inner Wisdom?

Whole group

SAY: Ego sure does try to capture our attention, doesn't it? Most of us hear a lot of that mind chatter in our heads, and sometimes it pulls us into negativity.

We may not be so used to listening for our own inner wisdom ... our intuition ... our gut instinct ... that still small voice that speaks only the truth. It's generally much more subtle and it takes our attention to notice it.

ASK: After reading about the differences between ego and our inner wisdom, who would be willing to share which channel they've tuned into in the past—their ego channel or their inner wisdom channel—and what the result has been?

–   Encourage at least one person to talk about being influenced by ego's negativity and one who will share about listening to their inner guidance.

✓ TIP

- If the group is large, ask people to limit their sharing to 2-3 min. to leave time for others to share.
- If people are hesitant to begin, be ready with your own story to get things started.

---

* Choose one or two of the questions (p.26-28) for participants to share in small groups.

Small group discussion (2-4 people)

Ask the participants to get into groups of 2-4 to share their answers to the question(s).

* (Depending upon the group size and whether you chose one or two questions, choose the appropriate amount of time for sharing between 10-40 minutes.)

SAY: You have*_____ (10-40) minutes. Kindly make sure that those who speak up easily make time for those who tend to be quieter. If you are one who tends to stay quiet, use this time to stretch a bit out of your comfort zone and let your thoughts be heard.

I will let you know when there are 5 minutes left. Are there any questions?

Whole group discussion

If time, ask everyone to share one thing that came up for them in the small group discussion, reminding everyone to bring up their thoughts only, not what someone else said.

- If time is limited, ask for 2-3 volunteers to share.
- If time is extremely limited, this part can be omitted.

Whole group

SAY: Now it's time to take a look at the Try This section on page 28.

SAY: You were invited to find pictures or draw what fear-based ego-negativity feels like, and then to do the same with what faith-based optimism feels like. You were then to ask yourself, "Which one do I want more of in my life? What do I intend to do about it?"

ASK: Who would be willing to share what came up for you with the two questions:

– Which one do I want more of in my life?

– What do I intend to do about it?

✧   Have volunteers share.

Closing

Have each person share one thing they are grateful for about themselves.

CHAPTER FOUR

Pretend Your Higher Power is Real

Whole group

SAY: In this chapter Jane asks us to accept that the God of our understanding is real, even if we can't sense its presence. She encourages us to pretend that it's right where we are all the time. We can to talk to it as if it hears us—because it does!

ASK: Who would be willing to share one way that they connect with the God of their understanding?

    ✧ Have volunteers share.

_____

✓ TIP

    • If people are hesitant to begin, be ready with your own example to get things started.

_____

SAY: Jane also asks us to understand the power of our own creative mind.

ASK: *How can we use our creative mind to help us begin to deepen our relationship with our Higher Power?* (What we believe becomes true for us, act as if, use our imaginations, pretend)

    ✧ Have volunteers share.

* Choose one or two of the questions (p.34-35) for participants to share in small groups.

Small group discussion (2-4 people)

Ask the participants to get into groups of 2-4 to share their answers to the question(s).

* **(Depending upon the group size and whether you chose one or two questions, choose the appropriate amount of time for sharing between 10-40 minutes.)**

SAY: You have*_____ (10-40) minutes. Kindly make sure that those who speak up easily make time for those who tend to be quieter. If you are one who tends to stay quiet, use this time to stretch a bit out of your comfort zone and let your thoughts be heard.

I will let you know when there are 5 minutes left. Are there any questions?

Whole group discussion

If time, ask everyone to share one thing that came up for them in the small group discussion.

- – If time is limited, ask for 2-3 volunteers to share.
- – If time is extremely limited, this part can be omitted.

Whole group

SAY: Now it's time to take a look at the Try This section on page 35.

SAY: You were encouraged to make a list of 10 attributes that define your Higher Power—truths that you want to experience from the God of your understanding.

ASK: Who will share one of the attributes that defines the God of your understanding, and tell us how it has shown up in your life?

- ✦ Have volunteers share.

_____

✓ TIP

- • Be ready to get the conversation started by sharing from your own experience.

_____

Closing

Have each person share one thing they're grateful for about the God of their understanding. Example:

"I'm grateful that the God of my understanding hears me," or "I'm grateful to be learning that the God of my understanding accepts me, just as I am."

CHAPTER FIVE

Become Willing to Trust

Whole group

SAY: This chapter is all about becoming willing to trust. Becoming willing to do anything is a powerful first step toward action! The step we're asked to take here is to trust that we live in a friendly universe that wants us to succeed.

SAY: In this chapter Jane talks about getting her first pair of glasses and seeing through new eyes.

ASK: Think back to the last few years of your life; what is one way have you started to see the world through new eyes? Offer the following suggestions:

- Starting to look for what's right instead of what's wrong
- Less complaining
- Not taking things so personally
- Finding more to be grateful for
- Being kinder to others
- Being kinder to yourself
- Becoming more patient

✧ Have volunteers share.

_____

✓ TIP

- If people are hesitant to begin, be ready to get things started with one way you've started to see through new eyes.

_____

* Choose one or two of the questions (p.41-43) for participants to share in small groups.

Small group discussion (2-4 people)

Ask the participants to get into groups of 2-4 to share their answers to the question(s).

* (Depending upon the group size and whether you chose one or two questions, choose the appropriate amount of time for sharing between 10-40 minutes.)

Say: You have*_____ (10-40) minutes. Kindly make sure that those who speak up easily make time for those who tend to be quieter. If you are one who tends to stay quiet, use this time to stretch a bit out of your comfort zone and let your thoughts be heard.

I will let you know when there are 5 minutes left. Are there any questions?

Whole group discussion

If time, ask everyone to share one thing that came up for them in the small group discussion.

- – If time is limited, ask for 2-3 volunteers to share.
- – If time is extremely limited, this part can be omitted.

Whole group

Say: Now it's time to take a look at the Try This section on pages 43 and 44.

Say: You've been working with an affirmation that's personal to you, or the one offered in the workbook.

Ask: Who would be willing to share their affirmation and how it's changing your life?

✧ Have volunteers share.

_____

✓ TIP

- • Be ready to get the conversations started by sharing from your own experience.

_____

Closing

Have each person share one thing they're grateful for about how their life is changing.

CHAPTER SIX

Understanding Spiritual Laws

Whole group

SAY: In this chapter spiritual laws are explained. We learned that they work automatically, just like the physical laws of gravity, mathematics or aerodynamics. Also like physical laws, they work the same for everyone. When we understand how they work, spiritual laws are reminders that our minds are very powerful creators!

SAY: Jane explains that what we think about becomes true for us. If our thoughts are mostly positive, good things tend to come our way. If our thoughts are mostly negative, then negative people and situations make their way to us.

When a challenge occurs, we are at choice as to how to look at it—as something awful or an opportunity to be the person we want to be—both of which are creative.

The good news is that once we begin to change the way we think, speak and act, our lives change.

ASK: How have you seen the Law of Cause and Effect, Law of Attraction, or Law of Circulation at work in your life?

   ✧   Have volunteers share.

_____

✓ *TIP*

•   If people are hesitant to begin, be ready with your own experience of spiritual laws to get things started.

_____

* Choose one or two of the questions (p.50-51) for participants to share in small groups.

Small group discussion (2-4 people)

Ask the participants to get into groups of 2-4 to share their answers to the question(s).

* (Depending upon the group size and whether you chose one or two questions, choose the appropriate amount of time for sharing between 10-40 minutes.)

SAY: You have*_____ 10-40 minutes. Kindly make sure that those who speak up easily make time for those who tend to be quieter. If you are one who tends to stay quiet, use this time to stretch a bit out of your comfort zone and let your thoughts be heard.

I will let you know when there are 5 minutes left. Are there any questions?

Whole group discussion

If time, ask everyone to share one thing that came up for them in the small group discussion.

- If time is limited, ask for 2-3 volunteers to share.
- If time is extremely limited, this part can be omitted.

Whole group

SAY: Now it's time to take a look at the Try This section on page 52.

ASK: What's one thing that makes you happy that you do as often as possible?

_____

✓ TIP

- Try to save enough time to have everyone share—this should go pretty quickly, and hearing different ideas often triggers positive, "I like that, too!" responses that others will relate to.
- If participants hear something that's true for them also, they can add it to their list.
- Be ready to get the conversations started by sharing one thing that makes you happy that you do often.
- If there's not enough time, just have a few volunteers share.

Closing

Have each person choose a different activity (other than the one they shared) that makes them happy and close with gratitude for this activity.

CHAPTER SEVEN

Peeling the Onion Sometimes Makes You Cry

Whole group

SAY: Peeling away the layers of the onion of our lives, each layer bringing us to the sweetness in the middle, is generally an eye-opening experience! Rarely is it easy. It asks us to accept and love each part of ourselves, including the feelings and negative thoughts we've been trying to avoid.

ASK: What is one thing have you discovered about yourself in the process of peeling back the onion that is you?

✧   Have volunteers share.

_____

✓ *TIP*

- If people are hesitant to begin, be ready with your own experience to get things started.

_____

* Choose one or two of the questions (p.58-59) for participants to share in small groups.

Small group discussion (2-4 people)

Ask the participants to get into groups of 2-4 to share their answers to the question(s).

* (Depending upon the group size and whether you chose one or two questions choose the appropriate amount of time for sharing between 10-40 minutes.)

SAY: You have*_____ (10-40) minutes. Kindly make sure that those who speak up easily make time for those who tend to be quieter. If you are one who tends to stay quiet, use this time to stretch a bit out of your comfort zone and let your thoughts be heard.

I will let you know when there are 5 minutes left. Are there any questions?

Whole group discussion

If time, ask everyone to share one thing that came up for them in the small group discussion.

  – If time is limited, ask for 2-3 volunteers to share.

  – If time is extremely limited, this part can be omitted.

Whole group

Say: Now it's time to take a look at the Try This section on pages 60 and 61.

Say: This was your opportunity to contemplate where you are in the process of peeling away the layers of the onion to discover that bright light within you.

  Are you at the very beginning . . .
  the outside of the onion . . .
  still thinking about peeling back the first layer?
  Have you gotten to the first layer, just beginning the discovery process?

Where are you?

_____

✓ TIP

  • Be ready to get the conversations started by pointing out where you are in peeling back the layers of the onion that is you.

_____

  ✧ Have volunteers share.

Closing

Have each person share one thing they're grateful for about themselves as they peel back the onion that is *them*. (For instance: I'm grateful for my tenacity. I'm grateful for my willingness to look at negative feelings. I'm grateful for realizing I'm more courageous than I thought I was.)

CHAPTER EIGHT

Choosing Happiness

Whole group

SAY: We all want to be happy, don't we? Why wouldn't we choose it? In this chapter we are asked to explore what it means to consciously choose happiness in each situation.

ASK: Who would be willing to describe a challenging time when they made the decision to move toward happiness instead of staying in the drama of the moment?

     ✧   Have volunteers share.

_____

✓ TIP

     • If people are hesitant to begin, once again begin the conversation with your example.

_____

* Choose one or two of the questions (p.66-68) for participants to share in small groups.

Small group discussion (2-4 people)

ASK the participants to get into groups of 2-4 to share their answers to the question(s).

* Depending upon the group size and whether you chose one or two questions, choose the appropriate amount of time for sharing between 10-40 minutes.)

SAY: You have*_____ (10-40) minutes. Kindly make sure that those who speak up easily make time for those who tend to be quieter. If you are one who tends to stay quiet, use this time to stretch a bit out of your comfort zone and let your thoughts be heard.

I will let you know when there are 5 minutes left. Are there any questions?

Whole group discussion

If time allows, ask everyone to share one thing that came up for them in the small group discussion.

- If time is limited, ask for 2-3 volunteers to share.
- If time is extremely limited, this part can be omitted.

Whole group

SAY: Once again it's time to take a look at the Try This section on page 68.

SAY: Choose three of the simple things you're grateful for and be ready to share them.

- Try to save enough time to have everyone share.
- This should go pretty quickly, as each person is simply stating three things for which they are grateful, which can be done in one sentence:

"I'm grateful for _____, _____, and _____."

Hearing different gratitudes often reminds others that they like the same thing, too. They can then add it to their gratitude lists.

––––––––––––––––

✓ TIP

- If there's not enough time for everyone to share, just have a few volunteers share.
- Be ready to get the conversations started by sharing three simple things you're grateful for.

––––––––––––––––

Closing

Have each person share one simple thing they're grateful for that they didn't share in the last activity.

CHAPTER NINE

Divine Discontent

Whole group

SAY: Divine discontent shows up when it's time to make a change. It's not meant to be comfortable; otherwise we'd still be doing what we were doing twenty years ago.

ASK: Who would be willing to tell about a time when divine discontent got you moving in a new direction?

✧ Have volunteers share.

– If people are hesitant to begin, be ready with your own story to get things started.

* Choose one or two of the questions (p.74-77) for participants to share in small groups.

Small group discussion (2-4 people)

Ask the participants to get into groups of 2-4 to share their answers to the question(s).

* (Depending upon the group size and whether you chose one or two questions, choose the appropriate amount of time for sharing between 10-40 minutes.)

SAY: You have*____ (10-40) minutes. Kindly make sure that those who speak up easily make time for those who tend to be quieter. If you are one who tends to stay quiet, use this time to stretch a bit out of your comfort zone and let your thoughts be heard.

I will let you know when there are 5 minutes left. Are there any questions?

Whole group discussion

If time, ask everyone to share one thing that came up for them in the small group discussion.

– If time is limited, ask for 2-3 volunteers to share.

– If time is extremely limited, this part can be omitted.

Whole group

Say: Now it's time to take a look at the Try This section on page 78.

Say: In this activity you were to choose one area that you want to change and then begin to celebrate each small step forward.

Ask: Who is willing to share what it is you're in the process of changing, as well as one thing you've done to move the process forward?

    ✧ Have volunteers share.

_____

✓ TIP

    • Be ready to get the conversations started by sharing from your own experience.

_____

Closing

Have each person share one thing they value most today and turn it into a statement of gratitude. For instance, "I'm grateful that I can speak up for myself."

Refer to page 75. In this section, the participants listed five things they value. They can choose one of those, or if something else came up as a result of the group discussion, they can choose that one.

CHAPTER TEN

Growing Your Faith

Whole group

SAY: In our time together we've moved forward in growing our faith.

SAY: Let's all share one way in which our faith has grown. (For instance: I'm more sure of myself in difficult situations; I'm starting to practice meditation; I'm starting to sense my Higher Power in my daily life; I'm kinder to myself and others; I'm more positive than I was before.)

SAY: As others share, you may see that same growth in yourself. If so, you can jot it down as a change within yourself.

✓ TIP

- This should go pretty quickly. Each person is stating one way in which their faith has grown in one or two sentences.
- If people are hesitant to begin, once again, be ready with an instance of your own growth in faith to get things started.

----

* Choose one or two of the questions for participants (p.83-85) to share in small groups.

Small group discussion (2-4 people)

Ask the participants to get into groups of 2-4 to share their answers to the question(s).

* (Depending upon the group size and whether you chose one or two questions choose the appropriate amount of time for sharing between 10-40 minutes.)

SAY: You have*_____ (10-40) minutes. Kindly make sure that those who speak up easily make time for those who tend to be quieter. If you are one who tends to stay quiet, use this time to stretch a bit out of your comfort zone and let your thoughts be heard.

I will let you know when there are 5 minutes left. Are there any questions?

Whole group discussion

If time allows, ask everyone to share one thing that came up for them in the small group discussion.

- – If time is limited, ask for 2-3 volunteers to share.
- – If time is extremely limited, this part can be omitted.

Whole group

SAY: As we begin to close out our time together, please turn to the What I Believe Could be Possible section beginning on page 88. (Then you read the following)

- • Today I believe the following could be possible about the God of my understanding.
- • Today I believe the following could be possible about me.
- • Today I believe the following could be possible about my life.

SAY: Please choose one of these statements and share one of your responses.

———————————————————

✓ TIP

- • Be sure to save enough time to have everyone share. It's important that every person is heard in order to validate the beliefs that are alive in their heart at this time in their lives.
- • You can ask participants to state it in one sentence so there will be time to hear from everyone.
- • Once again, as people listen to each other's sharing, it may generate an "Aha!" moment, "That's true for me, too!" in them.
- • Be ready to get the conversations started by sharing your own statement first, setting the tone for others to follow.

———————————————————

Closing

Have each person share one insight or revelation they've had as a result of this time together.

— Give everyone a moment to think of something before sharing begins.

If you're meeting in person, this is a good time to share hugs all around!

A Note to the Facilitator

I offer a heartfelt "Congratulations!" to you as you complete the facilitation of this workbook. Certainly it's been a growing experience for everyone involved and for you in particular as the facilitator. You've brought your own wisdom and experience to the facilitator position, creating an atmosphere in which everyone engaged in their own process of evolution.

Hopefully, you may wish to continue with the next two workbooks in this series, Part Two: and Part Three: , offering your services to those who continue to seek a greater relationship with the God of their understanding and themselves.

If you have any suggestions or questions, please don't hesitate to email me. I value your feedback!

With gratitude and love,

~ Jane

ABOUT

JANE BEACH

For the first fifty years of her life, Jane Beach was an atheist. In a moment of awareness, she discovered that God was real; her whole life changed, and much to her surprise, she became a minister! Jane's passion is her love affair with the one she calls the Beloved. Knowing what it feels like to live in a place of unconditional love and acceptance, she is committed to creating situations for others to do the same, relaxing into their own personal relationship with the God of their understanding. As Jane says, "Once you know how Loved you are, everything else takes care of itself."

Jane's writings invite readers to investigate their own love affair with the Divine . . . their own inner beauty. Her personal relationship life is contagious, and wherever she shows up an atmosphere of possibility, acceptance and unconditional love abound. A retreat facilitator, Jane has written twenty-five spiritual programs that are currently being taught in classes throughout the United States, Canada, the UK and Mexico included Centers for Spiritual Living, Unity, independent centers and the Institute of Noetic Sciences. Jane has recently retired as minister of the Conscious Living Center in Mountain View, California in order to take her message past its walls. She lives in Campbell, California.

You can email Jane at
revjanebeach@janebeach.com
Connect with her on Facebook® at
facebook.com/jane.beach.5

Visit Jane's author page on the publisher's website to learn about
forthcoming events, announcements and news.

About the Publisher

Kenos Press,™ an imprint of Six Degrees Publishing Group,™ publishes literary works which are meant to encourage and intimate connection with the Divine, uplift the human spirit, and further peace by improving our universal connection with one another. Learn more about Kenos Press at our link on the web at:
SixDegreesPublishing.com

www.ingramcontent.com/pod-product-compliance
Lightning Source LLC
LaVergne TN
LVHW061224060426
835509LV00012B/1415